FAITH THAT MAKES A DEMAND ON THE ANOINTING

Dr. Ed Dufresne

Ed Dufresne Ministries
Temecula, California

Unless otherwise indicated, all scriptural quotations are from the King James Version of the Bible.

Faith That Makes a Demand on the Anointing
Published by
Ed Dufresne Ministries
P.O. Box 186
Temecula, CA 92593
ISBN 0-940763-10-9

Copyright © 1996 by Dr. Ed Dufresne
All rights reserved.
Reproduction of text in whole or in part without the express written consent by the author is not permitted and is unlawful according to the 1976 United States Copyright Act.

Editorial Consultant: Phyllis Mackall
Printed in the United States of America.

Contents

Introduction 5

Chapter 1 ❧ The Touch of Faith 9

Chapter 2 ❧ Faith That Won't Give Up....................................15

Chapter 3 ❧ The Righteousness of God 23

Chapter 4 ❧ How Jesus Operated His Faith 31

Chapter 5 ❧ Faith Will Produce Every Time 35

Chapter 6 ❧ The Importance of Saying the Word 43

Chapter 7 ❧ When the Glory Shows Up 49

Chapter 8 ❧ Understanding the Prophet's Mantle....................55

Chapter 9 ❧ Making a Demand on the Prophet's Anointing....65

Conclusion 75

INTRODUCTION

All that will count is what you do for God.

Many people in the family of God go overboard in worldly pleasures and leave God out. They buy boats, campers, and other things, and there is nothing wrong with that — it's not a sin to do so — but they get so caught up in their activities, they find themselves too busy for the things of God.

How would you like to get to heaven, stand before Jesus, and be empty-handed? You might try to excuse yourself by saying, "Well, Lord, I caught a hundred fish one weekend — but I was with my family."

"How many souls did you win for Me?"

"But, Lord, I was busy. You know, I had these problems. I had these bills to pay."

But all that counts is what you do for God. That's the only thing you've got. As we get closer to the end-time revival, especially in the next few years, when the Church of the '90s is going to excel and be so powerful, there are going to be churches that will miss it. Why? Because they're going to be off doing something else! They're going to say, "This is what we want to do. We're going to follow our own plan. God, this is our plan, so bless it."

No, that's not the way it works.

Faith That Makes a Demand on the Anointing

Be in the Right Place

I like the story of Elisha. There were 50 prophets in this certain Bible school, the school of the prophets, and they said to him, "Don't you know that your master, Elijah, is going home today?"

Even they knew it by the Spirit. They knew it by the Spirit even though they stood afar off! They hadn't even crossed the river to where Elijah and Elisha were, yet they knew it!

And Elisha said, "Shut up. I know it."

What did he mean by that? Elisha was in the right position when that double portion fell on him. And those 50 other prophets knew it by the Spirit. You can know something is about to happen, but you can still miss it if you're not in the right position.

I've been telling churches across the nation, "Get in the right position. Get where God wants you to be, and make certain you're doing what He told you to do and you're willng to flow with the Spirit." All I can do is say it. Preachers, to get in the right position, do whatever it takes, even if you have to sell everything you've got.

After the double portion fell on Elisha, and Elijah went up into heaven in the fiery chariot, those 50 prophets asked, "Where's Elijah?" And they went looking for his body.

That's the way it's going to be in a lot of dead churches today. They're going to go back and look at the past. They're going to say, "Remember how God used to move in our midst in days gone by? Lord, remember 1907, 1940, and 1947?"

Like the 50 prophets in the Old Testament, they will be out looking for that which is dead, the wave that is gone. But I want you to know there is a new wave, and we need to be in the right position, church, to ride on the crest of it.

I don't want to be asleep when that changing of God occurs. I want to be in the right position to get the portion God has for me. Churches need to have this attitude as well.

The Unwelcome Guest

This reminds me of a story about a black preacher. A white pastor heard him singing on the radio and invited him to his church. He said, "We have a church of 5,000. Would you come and sing for us?"

Introduction

He said, "Yes, I'll come."

The pastor didn't know his guest was black. His church was down South.

The guest flew in, rented a car, went to the hotel, and then drove to the church that Sunday morning. When he walked up to the church, one of the ushers said, "Where are you going, sir?"

He said, "Well, I'm going to this church. I'm going to sing."

The usher said, "No, you're not. We don't allow black people in our church."

"Well, you're mistaken. Your pastor invited me. I have the letter right here in my briefcase." He showed the invitation to the usher.

And he said, "I don't understand this. Let's go around to the back and go into the pastor's study."

As they walked into the pastor's study, the usher said, "Pastor, this is Mr. So-and-so whom you invited to sing this morning."

The pastor looked up and said, "Oh, no. Oh, no. I'm sorry, but we don't allow black people in our church."

The guest replied, "But you *invited* me. I flew in, just as you told me to."

The pastor said, "Well, I'm sorry, but we just don't allow black people in this church." And he opened the door and said, "You may leave now." He let him out and shut the door. This black brother stood outside crying. He said, "Lord, they won't allow me in this church."

The Lord said, "Son, I've been trying to get in there for 30 years, and they won't let Me in, either!"

Chapter One

THE TOUCH OF FAITH

> *And they came to Jericho: and as he went out of Jericho with his disciples and a great number of people, blind Bartimaeus...sat by the highway side begging.*
>
> MARK 10:46

Bartimaeus was a different kind of beggar. His style of begging, the Bible says, was "importune." In other words, he wouldn't take no for an answer!

I've been around the usual kind of beggars, but I've also been around others who just won't leave you alone until you give them money. Have you ever been around people like that? You finally give them what they want because they just won't leave you alone!

That's what we ought to do with our faith. If you read the whole story, you'll find that Jesus said this beggar had faith.

He engaged in a different kind of begging: Bartimaeus had faith!

> *And when he heard that it was Jesus of Nazareth, he began to cry out, and say, Jesus, thou son of David, have mercy on me!*
>
> MARK 10:47

Say, "JESUS! Have mercy on me!"

You can say that in faith. I have many times. As much as I fly, I have to. Many times on airplanes, I've cried out, "Jesus!"

Calling on That Name

I heard some people give an amazing testimony once on this very subject.

Faith That Makes a Demand on the Anointing

They were driving down the street, and a truck coming toward them suddenly went out of control. There was no doubt they were going to be involved in a head-on collision with it.

As that truck sped toward them, they cried, "JESUS!" After a split second of time, almost like a flash of light, they looked in the rear view mirror of their car, and the truck was still in their lane — but it was *behind* them. It had *passed through them*, metal through metal, yet there was no wreck. Glory to God!

This kind of faith will get things done!

Bartimaeus cried, *"Have mercy on me. And many charged him that he should hold his peace..."* (verses 47, 48).

The Living Bible brings it down to where we live: "'Shut up!' some of the people yelled at him. But he only shouted the louder, again and again....'"

The Trouble With Holy Places

I've been to Israel several times. Once God told me to go with Dr. Lester Sumrall. He said, "I want to speak to you there." God spoke to Dr. Sumrall about buying a cargo plane and feeding the poor. He also told him that certain men, myself included, were to be involved in the project. All of this happened in Jerusalem, where we held services the first three nights.

Then we went down to the Sea of Galilee, where Jesus did 80 to 85 percent of His miracles. This is my favorite spot in Israel. I especially like the town of Capernaum, where Peter's house was, and where Jesus healed Peter's mother-in-law.

There are two churches in this town, and the old church was built by the Crusaders on top of the original synagogue where Jesus preached. You can still see some pillars and stones from that synagogue on the side. Restoration work is in progress. The back wall is up, and they were working on the front wall, where the doors are, when we were there. The side walls were not rebuilt yet.

There were almost 600 people in the whole tour, and there were about 100 in the buses we were traveling with.

The Healing Jesus

As we stood inside that synagogue, a pastor and I started talking about the miracle power of Jesus. We started talking about the

The Touch of Faith

healing anointing, and the fact that Jesus still heals today.

Everyone was agreeing and praising the Lord with us, so the pastor asked the people, "How many of you have been healed by the power of God?" Nearly everyone raised his or her hand. He said, "All right, let's have some testimonies. Ma'am, what happened to you?"

The woman replied, "I had cancer, and I went to such-and-such a meeting. The power of God hit me and burned all that cancer out, and they didn't have to do any surgery on me." We got happy about that!

Then a man raised his hand and said, "I'm sixty-some years old. My heart was worn out, and the doctors said I'd be dead within just a few days, but I believed God and the power of God hit me and gave me a brand-new heart." The people began to praise and worship God, and they got loud about it.

We went around to five or six more people, praising and worshipping God after hearing their testimonies, and all of a sudden a man in an old robe ran inside and said, "Shhh! Shhh! Be quiet! Shut up! This is a *holy* place. This is *holy!*"

I looked around and said, "All I see is a bunch of rocks." (I don't have a religious spirit in me.)

It's amazing. Sometimes if you install just a few stained-glass windows in a church, the people almost worship the windows. I'd tell them, "If you think they'll heal you, touch them. They won't heal you; you'll just have cold hands."

Jesus is the Healer. Jesus is the Healer! He is the One who heals today.

An Invasion of Religious Spirits

That priest came in there and said, "Shut up!" And, of course, that was their church, so we had to abide by their rules, and we did. But God spoke to me. He said, "That's what is happening in many churches today."

He said, "The devil is coming in with religious spirits and telling them, 'Shhh. None of that stuff on Sunday morning now. We don't want any of that Charismatic, Holy Ghost, Full Gospel, Pentecostal, or even Word of Faith stuff.'"

Unfortunately, it's true. "We have 45 minutes of teaching," the pastors explain. "We've got two services, you know. Sister So-and-so has five minutes to sing a song. Run them in and run them out. And no moving of the Holy Ghost."

God said the devil is telling people to shut up. Of course, there are different ways to tell you to shut up. People usually don't come right in your face and say, "Shut up." Well, some tell me that.

I've gone to churches where I was supposed to have a week-long meeting, but it lasted only two days. People started getting healed, and the Lord started to "read their mail." The pastor had sin in his life and didn't like that. He said, "We're going to ask you to leave. We don't flow together." I said, "That's obvious."

Afraid of the Media

Recently, secular television shows have been telling Full Gospel people to shut up. I know preachers right now who are selling their large houses and buying much smaller ones because they are afraid of what the media will say. And they're watching their messages now, again because they fear what the media will say. I don't care what the media says. I'm not ashamed of the Gospel. I'm not ashamed of the healing Jesus.

We've said there are different streams of healing, but I want you to know there is only *one* stream, and it's from a healing Jesus. He is the Healer. He is the Baptizer. And He is the Deliverer.

There are many ways the devil is trying to tell the church to shut up and back off. I'm not backing off; I'm going to get stronger.

When it comes to the devil, I'm going to get stronger. I'm not shutting up, and I'm not backing off; I'm moving on. I'm going to be in the right position, and when this wind really gets blowing, I want to be right in the middle of it. I want to be right on the top of the wave.

Don't Compromise

Let's not compromise our message of faith and what the Word of God says. If Jesus said He's the Healer, He's the Healer. If God said He wants you to prosper, He wants you to prosper. By this, I don't mean wasting money; I mean having enough to take care of all your needs and more to give to the work of God. I don't mean everyone will become a millionaire.

A man once gave me a brand-new 1985 Mercedes. And one preacher said, "You'd better get rid of that car."

The Touch of Faith

"Why?" I asked. "I've been traveling around for twenty-some years for Jesus, and He just wanted to bless me. If God wants me to give the car to someone else, I will."

Stingy Spirits

I've given away two twin-engine airplanes when God said, "Give it to that preacher." I gave them the key. How many people would do that? Not many. Why? Because they've got stingy spirits.

There are people in churches that don't even pay their tithes.

"Well, Brother Ed, that passed away."

You've been listening to a religious devil telling you to shut up and saying, "Don't you give any money to that church. You don't know what they're going to do with it."

It's none of your business what the church does with your money. If you give it to the Lord, whoever spends the money is the one who is going to have to stand before God and give an account of his stewardship.

Justification for an Airplane

While I still owned the second twin-engine airplane, I used it to fly to a certain town to hold meetings. After one service, as I was leaving, a woman came up to me, grabbed me, and said, "Sir, I want to talk to you."

She said, "What justifies your having a twin-engine airplane?"

Her question caught me off guard, but out of my spirit I said, "Does your mayor have an airplane?"

She said, "As a matter of fact, he does, but he's the mayor of this city, and he has to get around."

I said, "Well, honey, I want you to know that I'm an ambassador for God. I have orders from God, and I have to get around, too. I'll tell you what justifies that airplane: one soul. One soul is worth more than anything on the face of this earth."

Stingy spirits don't like to hear that!

Benefits of Tithing

You who don't pay your tithes — do you want to know why your washing machine is always breaking down? Do you want to

Faith That Makes a Demand on the Anointing

know why you're always having problems? It's because you don't keep your "premiums" paid up.

You've got enough sense to pay your insurance, so that if anything happens, you're covered. But in regard to tithing, you're not covered when you don't keep your tithe premiums paid up.

"Well, that's under the old law."

Would you take Jesus' word for it in the New Testament?

He said, "It is better for you to have a millstone tied around your neck than to offend one of these little ones." Read it in Luke 15, 16, and 17.

In these chapters, Jesus is discussing your being a good steward, and He's talking about one who leaves the fold and goes out into sin.

He said, "When you're not a good steward of your money, you are offending one of those little ones out there in your community — one of those who are lost — by not helping with your money, your tithes and your offerings. You're offending the sinners in this community because you don't have the money to do the job God told you to do. You're holding it back."

He said, "It's better for you to have a millstone around your neck than to offend one of these little ones." Have you ever seen one of those millstones over in Israel? They're *huge*. If you were thrown into a lake with a millstone like that tied around you, you'd go straight to the bottom!

I'm not shutting up when it comes to the Word of God. As a matter of fact, I'm going to get *stronger* and *bolder* when it comes to the Word. I'm not compromising, I'm going to get everything that belongs to me — everything that my big Brother Jesus, my Savior — provided on Calvary. I'm going to walk in that.

Chapter 2

FAITH THAT WON'T GIVE UP

What if a famous, macho movie star knocked on your door and demanded, "I want you out of this house in three minutes! Take all your clothes with you. I'm taking everything you've got — your wife, your children, and your bank account." What would you do?

I'll tell you what *I'd* do. I'd say, "You and what army?"

That's what we're supposed to do when the devil knocks on our door and announces, "I've got some cancer for your family. I've got some poverty for your family."

Instead of replying, "Oh, come on in," it's time we were men. It's time we quit being whimps and stand up and say, "My Bible says this, and I will not be ashamed of the Gospel!"

(You young girls who aren't married yet, don't marry a whimp. Marry a tongue-talking, healing-believing, devil-casting-out man who won't shut up about the Gospel!)

Some of you go to church only on Sunday mornings, and you're backslidden and don't even know it. There are different ways to shut up. For example, most Full Gospel Christians are even afraid to pray out loud, such as saying grace in a restaurant.

Smith Wigglesworth wasn't afraid to pray in public. When he was ready to say grace in a restaurant, he'd ask all the other diners to be quiet, and then he'd pray. I'm not telling you to do that, but it's pretty bold. His friends report that everyone bowed their heads.

When the devil knocks at my door, I say, "Mr. Devil, you aren't having my wife. You aren't having my children. You aren't having

Faith That Makes a Demand on the Anointing

my finances. And you aren't having my health! Get out of here, in the Name of Jesus! You have no right around here. I keep my premiums paid up!"

Bartimaeus Wouldn't Shut Up

And many charged him that he should hold his peace: but he cried the more a great deal, Thou son of David, have mercy on me.

MARK 10:48

Blind Bartimaeus wouldn't shut up. I don't like the word *The Living Bible* uses here, but it makes it real: "'You lucky fellow,' they said 'come on, he's calling you.'"

That's amazing! One minute the crowd was telling him to shut up, and the next minute, after they saw that Jesus had stopped for him, they changed their attitude toward Bartimaeus.

Maybe they call you a "religious fanatic," but when they see healings taking place all around you, everyone you pray for gets healed and delivered, and God takes care of all of your needs, they'll change their attitude about you.

Give Jesus first place in your life. Put Jesus first in your home. Put Jesus first in your office. Put Jesus first in your finances. Put Jesus first in every area of your life!

Jesus Stopped for Faith

Bartimaeus wouldn't shut up. The story continues:

And Jesus stood still, and commanded him to be called....

MARK 10:49

I like that. I'm not shutting up when it comes to the Word of God. If it's in the Word, I'm going to believe it. I don't care if it hairlips the devil; I'm going to do what God told me to do. I will not shut up!

How would you like to be commanded by Jesus to come to Him? It reminds me of a game my little boy and I play. I'll chase Stephen around the house until I get tired. Then I'll sit down, and he'll say, "Get me, Daddy! Get me!"

I say that all the time to God. "God, get me! Get me, get me, get me!"

Faith That Won't Give Up

"Thy Faith Hath Made Thee Whole"

> ...And they call the blind man, saying unto him, Be of good comfort, rise; he calleth thee.
>
> And he, casting away his garment, arose, and came to Jesus.
>
> And Jesus answered and said unto him, What wilt thou that I should do unto thee? The blind man said unto him, Lord, that I might receive my sight.
>
> And Jesus said unto him, Go thy way; **thy faith hath made thee whole.** And immediately he received his sight, and followed Jesus in the way.
>
> MARK 10:49-52

Notice Jesus said that type of begging was *faith*. Do you understand what that kind of faith is?

First, blind Bartimaeus set a goal that he was going to get to Jesus. You must understand that he looked at Jesus in that era differently from the way we do today. He looked at Jesus as a prophet of God, because he knew the mantle that was on Him.

So did the woman with the issue of blood. She said, "If I may touch but His clothes, I shall be whole" (Mark 5:28). Another translation says, "If I may touch His mantle, I shall be whole."

The Touch of Faith

In the Old Testament, people used to go to the prophet and make a demand on his mantle or anointing.

You remember the story in Second Kings 4 of the Shunammite woman whose child died. He was out in the fields with his father when he suffered a sun stroke. His father carried him into the house and placed him in his mother's lap.

She, in turn, lay the dead child on the bed in the chamber reserved for the prophet Elisha, who stayed at their home when he was in the vicinity. She said, "I'll be back," and she set off to seek the prophet of God.

The Bible says, "When you receive a prophet in the name of a prophet, you receive a prophet's reward" (Matthew 10:41). God told me the reward this woman received 16 years later — her child being raised from the dead — was because she took care of the prophet.

So the people in Bible days looked at Jesus differently, because He was then walking under the Abrahamic Covenant as a prophet. Although He was the Savior, too, they didn't understand that yet. However, they knew how to make a demand on a prophet. They knew that the prophet had a healing anointing or mantle.

Be like blind Bartimaeus, who locked in on Jesus, the prophet of God. *Lock in to the will of God for your life, and don't shut up or give up.* Don't let religious people keep you from worshipping God in supposed "holy" places.

Keep Your Eyes on Jesus

I am listening to the Word; I am not listening to the news that comes and goes. Jesus is the same yesterday, today, and forever. If people fell because of different things that happened to some of our leaders in recent years, it means they had their eyes on man and not on Jesus.

Men will fail you. Your pastor can only do so much, but there's a Jesus who passed His test. If you want an example to follow, follow after Jesus. Go back into the gospels and see how He handled everything. He used the Word of God. He's my example; not men.

God does use men, and there are areas where we give men honor, but we're to give Jesus *all* the honor.

"Well, I heard about this man. They say he did this, and he did that."

That's just the devil trying to get you to shut up your convictions and what you believe. Believe in Jesus. Depend on Jesus. Don't depend on me to get your healing, because I don't have it. *He who is in me is the One who does the healing.*

It is extremely important that we all be in the right position. Let's get in our position. Let's find out the will of God. Let's quit drifting around, just sitting in church and taking all the time. Let's start giving of our finances, our time, and everything else. Let's find out what the will of God is for us and then don't shut up. Just stay in there.

"Brother Ed, I need healing."

Then start studying the Bible about healing, and find out what the will of God is for you concerning healing. You've got to build your own faith up, lock in on it, and don't give up until you get it. Stay right in there, confessing, "It is written."

Faith That Won't Give Up
My Household Shall Be Saved

My dad has gone home to be with the Lord, but my daddy had been an alcoholic all his life, and he tried to die on me five different times. But every time he'd get ready to die, something would happen, and the doctors just didn't understand it.

They didn't know it, but it was because I have a covenant with my heavenly Father to believe on the Lord Jesus Christ and I shall be saved — *and my household.*

Every time my daddy got seriously ill, he'd say, "Now, don't phone little Eddie." That's what he called me. He hadn't realized that I became big Eddie. In his eyes, I was still little Eddie. He'd say, "Don't you phone him."

I'd be in a hotel room and the Spirit of God would tell me, "Your dad's in trouble. Give him a call."

When Dad would answer, he'd ask, "How did you find out?" Then he'd stop and answer it himself: "Oh, I know. That Holy Ghost told you. Will you let me die in peace?"

I'd say, "No, not until you give your heart to Jesus."

When I was preaching in San Bernardino a few years ago, I saw my dad come in the back of the church and sit down. He had a big beard. I said, "That's my dad!"

I had phoned him and asked him to come, but he had said, "Nope." When he says nope, that's it. But he came. He was raised a Catholic. He only stayed in church long enough to put his dollar in the basket once a year and light a candle.

But he sat in my meeting for three hours. He raised his hands like the others, and when I prayed for everyone in the building who wanted to be saved to raise their hands, he raised his hands and prayed with me. Glory! I just refused to give up on him.

The devil had been beating me over the head with the fact that my dad wasn't saved. "You're traveling all over the world, and your dad isn't even saved!"

I would say, "You lying devil! I've got a covenant with my heavenly Father to believe on the Lord. If I didn't believe in Him, I wouldn't be running all over the country, preaching. I'd get a 9 to 5 job, buy a camper and a boat, and have vacations and be like everyone else."

In Love With Jesus

But I'm in love with Jesus. I can't stop traveling. I've got a burning in my heart to preach. In fact, I'm doubling up on my meetings. It just burns in my spirit that time is so short, and what we do for Jesus is all that's going to count.

We're seeing one of the greatest revivals in history starting to take place, a little bit here and a little bit there. We're in it. It's going to be the greatest revival the world has ever seen!

We're going to see more healings and more working of miracles than the world has seen since the Day of Pentecost. As a matter of fact, God has told me that this wave is going to be a combination of all the waves since Pentecost. All the history of all the waves is going to be in this one wave. Our church buildings won't be big enough to hold the harvest of people who are going to be saved.

Hospitals Will Be Emptied

Once there was a man by the name of John Alexander Dowie who ministered in Chicago around the turn of the century. He was arrested more than a hundred times in just one year for "practicing medicine without a license."

The medical industry was so angry at him for praying for the sick, they put lawsuits on him. God said that's what is going to happen in this next wave, because the hospitals are going to be emptied of their patients after they are healed!

The medical profession is going to put lawsuits on us, because most of their industry is geared by money and greed, anyway. Do you think they're trying to get a cure for AIDS because they truly love the homosexuals? No, they stand to make billions of dollars if they could get the treatment to cure the disease.

I predict we are going to see homosexuals come to our churches by the thousands if not the millions in this next wave, because the only way they are going to get healed is through divine healing.

They are going to have to repent of that sin and get delivered, and God will heal them.

I also predict that there are going to be a lot more diseases doctors won't have a cure for, and the only way people will be healed of them is to come to the church and look to a healing Jesus. I tell people, "Why don't you take the gos-pill?"

Learn the Will of God

I'm not shutting up about this. Bartimaeus heard that Jesus was walking by, and he didn't care; he was going to get to that Man. He was going to get what he went after.

That's what the Holy Spirit is saying to churches today. Find out the will of God, lock in on it, and then don't shut up. It doesn't matter what anyone says.

"Well, I don't know... I don't know if you should try that divine healing stuff. I don't know about that baptism in the Holy Spirit, and I don't know about trusting preachers. You know what happened."

If everyone in a church would pay his or her tithes every Sunday, the finances of that church would quadruple. The church would be able to reach out in television and other areas God has given them a vision for. They'd be able to build that new building God has put on their hearts.

A Dead Man's Reactions

The Bible says we are to give our body as a living sacrifice. What happens to a sacrifice? It's dead, so it doesn't care what anyone thinks about it. I tell my body that all the time.

It says, "You can't. You go too much. You're tired. You can't take that." I say, "Shut up, body. You're dead. Dead bodies don't gripe." Dead bodies don't gossip or get sick, either.

But understand, I don't go beyond wisdom regarding the care of my body. We do have to take proper care of our bodies.

My goal is to get people saved, healed, set free, and turned on to Jesus.

Chapter 3

THE RIGHTEOUSNESS OF GOD

And all thy children shall be taught of the Lord; and great shall be the peace of thy children.

In righteousness shalt thou be established.

ISAIAH 54:13,14

Many Christians are defeated in life because they haven't established the fact that they are the righteousness of God.

The way the devil defeats Christians is by beating them over the head with sin-consciousness all the time. He says things like, "You aren't anything but a dirty old sinner, and you're this and you're that — and remember the mistakes you made? God isn't going to answer *your* prayers!"

Do you know what I do when the devil tells me that? I look at myself in the mirror and say, "You righteous person, straighten up in the Name of Jesus! I am righteous, not by my choice, but by His choice."

Most Christians don't have all their spiritual armor on. One piece of the Christian's armor is the breastplate of righteousness. The Bible says in First Corinthians 1:30 that we are righteous because of what He did:

But of him are ye in Christ Jesus, who of God is made unto us wisdom, and righteousness, and sanctification, and redemption.

Jesus' Righteousness

I was saved in a Full Gospel church. They would always say, "Your righteousness is as filthy rags." The Bible also says in James

Faith That Makes a Demand on the Anointing

that a righteous man's prayers avail much, so if we were only righteous, we could get so much done. There's no doubt that our righteousness is as filthy rags, but I'm not referring to *my* righteousness; I'm referring to *His* righteousness and what He has provided for me.

Notice what it says in Isaiah 54:14: "In righteousness shalt thou be established." This is one of the most important things you need to establish in your Christian walk — that you are the righteousness of God.

Then, after you establish the fact that you are the righteousness of God, the passage continues:

...thou shalt be far from oppression; for thou shalt not fear: and from terror [fear is torment]; for it shall not come near thee.

ISAIAH 54:14

I go to a lot of churches, and a lot of people in those churches are depressed and oppressed. As a matter of fact, when I have healing lines, I say, "I want everyone who is oppressed and depressed to come up for prayer." Usually anywhere from 50 to 75 percent of the members come to the front for prayer.

When Depression Strikes

Preachers are not excluded from any of these attacks. Sometimes I get tempted to be depressed, too. If oppression or depression tries to get hold of me, I go right back to the Word of God and I continue to study.

I get the E.W. Kenyon book on righteousness or some good tapes on righteousness and go back through the scriptures and establish the fact in me that I am the righteousness of God; that I am in right-standing because of the blood of Jesus Christ.

And I examine myself to see if I have any sin in my life. If so, I get rid of it, because "If we confess our sins, he is faithful and just to forgive us our sins, and to cleanse us from all unrighteousness" (1 John 1:9).

You'll never fight the devil — you'll never fight sickness and disease, poverty, financial problems, or any of these things — until you establish the fact of who you are in Christ. You'll never stand up to the devil, because you don't know who you are!

And if you go to a lot of Full Gospel churches, you won't know who the bad guy is: God or the devil. The way they preach, you won't know which one is the enemy.

I know, because I got saved in a Full Gospel church. As a matter of fact, I got kicked out of it after I got a book called *Healing the Sick* by T. L. Osborn. It's dangerous to get a book like that, especially if you're hungry!

Look Out, Devil!

There's something about it when you find out who you are in Christ, and that the devil has lied to you all your life. Look out, devil! How many of you ever got fed up with his lies and said, "Enough is enough. Get out of here, devil" — and ran him off?

This passage from Isaiah 54:14 says, "You will be far from oppression." And the 17th verse says:

No weapon [or no instrument of war] that is formed against thee shall prosper; and every tongue that shall rise against thee in judgment thou shalt condemn. This is the heritage of the servants of the Lord, *and their righteousness is of me,* saith the Lord.

No weapon! Notice the subject here is righteousness.

I have a tape that is entitled *"Moses' Rod, Jesus."* It came about because I was thinking about the Name of Jesus, and I was thinking about the power of attorney that we have.

Just imagine the richest man in town coming to you and giving you the power of attorney to sign his name to any check you wanted and to take care of his affairs while he was gone. That's what Jesus did for you and me!

I started thinking about that, and it just came up in my spirit: "So it was with Moses, when he used that rod. The rod was his authority when he went before Pharaoh and said, 'Let my people go.'" Then, when Pharaoh's magicians produced rods that turned into snakes, Moses placed his rod on the ground — and it ate up the devil's serpents!

Use Your Authority on Your Problem

The Lord told me, *"That authority that split the Red Sea is the same authority you have in the Name of Jesus Christ!"* I don't know what your

Faith That Makes a Demand on the Anointing

problem is, but you can split it open with the Name of Jesus!

But first you've got to believe in that Name when you pray. And you can't believe it religiously, like a lot of people do. They pray religiously. To them, it's like using a "lucky" rabbit's foot. Furthermore, don't ask for what you want "for *Jesus'* sake." If it's for anyone's sake, it's for your sake. Jesus is doing fine. *He* doesn't need any help.

Five minutes after they pray, some people say, "O God, what are we going to do now?" They never believed what they prayed, and they didn't ask for their petition in Jesus' Name.

Jesus said, "...*Whatsoever ye shall ask in my name, that will I do*" (John 14:13). I like to preach on that text, too.

Something That Works

Now I'm going to teach you something the Lord has taught me through the years. It has always worked for me, in both rough times and good times. If you hear someone preach something, but it never works, what good is it?

I like things that *work*. I'd rather go to a John Wayne movie than listen to some preachers. Why? You know John Wayne is going to *win* every time, because he's the good guy! Listening to some preachers, you can't tell who's the good guy — God or the devil!

In Mark 10:46, we read:

And they came to Jericho: and as he went out of Jericho with his disciples and a great number of people, blind Bartimaeus ...sat by the highway side begging.

I call this "faith begging." It is a different kind of begging from the kind where someone sits motionless, puts his hand out, and cries, "Alms, alms."

The Faith God Honors

Bartimaeus' begging is characterized by "importunity." He's a man who went after something, and he didn't leave it alone until he got it. That's the kind of faith God honors. That's the kind of faith Jesus stopped for, and He asked, "What is it, that I can do for you?"

And the blind beggar said, "That I might receive my sight."

The Righteousness of God

Do you remember what Jesus said? "Thy faith hath made thee whole." It was not the begging or the yelling that got the blind man his sight; it was his faith.

Let's read on.

> *And when he heard that it was Jesus of Nazareth, he began to cry out, and say, Jesus, thou son of David, have mercy on me.*
>
> *And many charged him that he should hold his peace.*
>
> MARK 10:47,48

And as we saw, *The Living Bible* says, "They told him to shut up."

There are different ways for the devil to tell you to shut up; to get you to back off from what you're believing for. He'll say, "Don't trust preachers anymore. Don't believe God for your healing. Just shut up. Don't get carried away with all that faith stuff."

> *And many charged him that he should hold his peace: but he cried the more a great deal, Thou Son of David, have mercy on me.*
>
> *And Jesus stood still, and commanded him to be called.*
>
> MARK 10:48,49

I'd love it if Jesus commanded me, "Ed, come here. I want to talk to you." How would you like Jesus to call your name and command you to come to Him? Would you like that? *God always honors faith.*

Faith Speaks From a Coma

Years ago, when we first started our church, a woman started attending and got hold of the Word of God. She had been in a denominational Full Gospel church all her life.

As she and her husband were driving home after one of our services, the devil tried to kill her with a stroke. They rushed her to the hospital. She went into a coma. The doctors said, "We want to operate, we've got to dissolve her blood clot, but it doesn't look too good."

So they called me since I was their pastor. She was still in the emergency room. Her parents, who were raised in a Full Gospel denominational church, were falling apart. They were having a fit. Mind you, this whole family, generation after generation, had been raised in Full Gospel churches.

But this woman and her husband had been attending our

church, and we had been teaching them faith. We had been teaching them that it is God's will for them to be healed.

When I walked into the emergency room, I said, "What's the problem?" Even though she was in a coma, the woman heard my voice, and replied, "Brother Ed, give me the Word. I need the Word!"

The doctors jumped back and said, "How can she talk when she's in a coma."

A Carrier of the Word

And God said to me, "It's because your voice has delivered the Word to her so many months. You were the carrier of that Word to her spirit." She'd heard my voice all that time, listening to all my tapes.

I started quoting the Word of God to her. Right away, her parents almost pushed me out of that room. They were rude and said, "You're an occultist. Get out of here." But her husband said, "No, *you* get out of here. He is my pastor."

When I say, "Don't shut up with your faith," I'm talking about using your faith. I asked a woman from the church to take tapes of the New Testament and Brother Hagin's healing scriptures tape to the hospital and play them to the sick woman over and over again, night and day.

Full Gospel Unbelief

When the patient's father brought their Full Gospel pastor into that hospital room, they ran that woman off, threw the tape on the floor, and sat down and talked about politics.

Of course, when her husband came in the morning, he told the men, "I don't want you in this room at all!" That didn't make him very popular.

Don't forget: In the middle of a war, you're not trying to win a popularity contest. The devil will use your family and other loved ones to steal your miracle. That's true, and you know it. I'm going to prove it to you.

The woman recovered from her stroke and did not have to have an operation. God dissolved her blood clot. She was partially paralyzed in her leg and part of her arm for a few years after

The Righteousness of God

that. Then the doctors told her she could never have another child, but she did have another healthy child. Today she's in my son-in-law's church, still healed.

And I guarantee you, if she would have listened to those Full Gospel preachers, she would be dead today. Thank God for a husband who stood in the gap and didn't allow that to happen! I praise God for her healing.

Chapter 4

HOW JESUS OPERATED HIS FAITH

Now go over to John 11, which is the story of Lazarus. I want to show you how Jesus operated His faith. Maybe you've never heard this before, but God revealed something to me out of this story.

Now a certain man was sick, named Lazarus, of Bethany, the town of Mary and her sister Martha.

(It was that Mary which had anointed the Lord with ointment, and wiped his feet with her hair, whose brother Lazarus was sick.)

Therefore his sisters sent unto him saying, Lord, behold, he whom thou lovest is sick.

When Jesus heard that, he said, This sickness is not unto death, but for the glory of God, that the Son of God might be glorified thereby.

JOHN 11:1-4

It amazes me that even Full Gospel, Spirit-filled preachers read into this passage that Lazarus' sickness was supposed to be for the glory of God. I can't see how they read that in there.

What this passage does show us, however, is that the man's healing is for the glory of God. God never receives glory out of sickness, because He isn't the source of it. But He is the source of healing, so it is only in that, that He is glorified.

Many people are talking about preachers today. They say, "Oh, this one did this, and that one did that, and the media says such-and-such."

I know we ministers of the Gospel are supposed to be an example to the flock, but I don't follow after preachers. I follow after Jesus. Men have character flaws and make mistakes, but Jesus was

Faith That Makes a Demand on the Anointing

the Son of God, and He passed His test! He's our best example.

People have told me, "Well, I knew someone who believed in divine healing, and he died."

I'm not following after that person. I don't care if every person I pray for dies; I'm still going to believe in healing. And I'm *still* going to believe in Jesus, because He passed His test, and He's my example.

Deep Revelations

It amazes me that everyone wants *deep* revelations. "Yes, brother, we go to this group, and this guy's got a *deep* revelation."

Did you know that most Christians don't even have Mark 11:22-25 down yet? They say they don't want to hear this simple, basic stuff anymore, because they're into deep stuff now. But they don't even know Mark 11:22-25 yet! You can tell what they believe by what comes out of their mouths; by their confessions. Let me show you what Jesus did at Lazarus' grave. Actually, He was planting a seed by what He said. He said of Lazarus, "He will live and not die!" *He planted His faith when He said it with His mouth.* This is where a lot of people miss it.

When Jesus said, "He will live and not die" (literally, "This sickness is not unto death," verse 4), He was planting words as seeds into the spirit realm — and those words will produce for you every time.

Do you think you are better than Jesus? I don't think anyone would say that. If you are going to walk like Jesus walked, the devil is going to try to pull the same tricks on you that he tried to pull on Jesus. But if you get in the Word of God and learn how Jesus handled the devil, and if you learn that He has given us the power of attorney, you will win. Winning is the name of the game!

What Is God Going To Do?

Blind Bartimaeus won. He got his healing. If you watch John Wayne movies, you'll find he wins every time. But if you listen to some preachers, they say, "Well, sometimes you win and sometimes you don't. You never know what God is going to do."

Yes, I know what God is going to do: *He is going to do exactly what He said in His Word!*

How Jesus Operated His Faith

"Well, I know people who tried that, and it didn't work."

My faith isn't based on someone else's experience. I'm basing it on God. I believe in Him. He is the One who won't fail me. He has never failed me.

True Friends

Several years ago, I had two days to raise $136,000 or lose the option on my church building in Los Angeles. The banks wouldn't give me any money, and many of my friends dropped me like a hot potato.

It's amazing, when you've got your back up against the wall, how few friends you've got. And it's amazing, when it looks like you're finished, how many Christians will jump in with the devil and try to finish you off.

"Who's that guy you're stepping on?"

"Oh, he used to be my pastor. For 35 years he pastored my mother and daddy, he pastored me, and he pastored my children, but he made a mistake."

The devil was looking at my circumstances, thinking, "I've got to get that seed of faith out of Ed Dufresne's heart."

The Lord said to me, "No one — no devil, no angel, no one — can dig that seed up but you." *The one who planted his faith is the only one who can dig that seed up.* So you're the only one who can keep your faith from producing, because faith will produce for you.

It produced for blind Bartimaeus. People told him, "Be quiet. Don't you know that He is holy? Shut up!" But he just yelled the louder, and his faith stopped Jesus.

Every one of you has the measure of the God-kind of faith in you, and that seed will produce. All you have to do is plant it and use it. If you will not compromise, the glory of God will show up for you every time.

I've been through hard times and good times alike, so I'm talking about something I live; I'm not just preaching a sermon full of empty words.

Walking Faith

Someone asked me, "What is faith?"

Faith That Makes a Demand on the Anointing

I answered, "Look at Dr. Lester Sumrall. He doesn't preach faith; he *lives* faith. He is walking faith. Just follow him around, and you'll see what I mean.

God said to him, "Go buy that TV station." He didn't have a dime, but he signed the papers and bought the station. Don't attempt that unless you've got faith and a word from the Lord to base it on.

Many people talk a lot about faith, but they don't *live* it. There are a lot of hearers, but few *doers*. They hear the message, they say amen, and they yell the loudest — but they don't live it. I know, because I have pastored for 13 1/2 years.

Some of my people said, "Yes, amen. I believe it that way. Yea, glory!" Then tragedy hit, and they fell apart.

I've had a young man tell me, "You know, I got in the ministry, and my wife left me. I'm finished. That's it." That is a hurtful thing. Don't misunderstand me; I'm not making light of it. But the young man said, "I'm finished. That's it. God let me down."

I asked, "You're going to go to hell for a woman?" Or, "Lady, are you going to go to hell for a man because he took off with another woman?"

I know the breakup of a relationship is a hurtful thing — I'm not making light of it — but are you going to stop serving God because the devil came along and tried to destroy you? He was really trying to steal that Word in you. He was trying to steal that seed out of you.

Chapter 5

FAITH WILL PRODUCE EVERY TIME

When Jesus said in front of Lazarus' tomb, "He will live and not die," the devil said, "I've got to get Him off that subject!" Why? Because that seed of faith will produce every time, and the glory will show up. I'm going to show you how the resurrection power will show up at your house. Let's read on:

Now Jesus loved Martha, and her sister, and Lazarus.

When he had heard therefore that he was sick, he abode two days still in the same place where he was.

JOHN 11:5,6

Do you know something? *Faith never gets nervous.* Jesus stayed where He was for two more days, knowing Lazarus would die.

Then after that saith he to his disciples, Let us go unto Judaea again.

JOHN 11:7

Jesus said that. If Jesus says something, will you believe it? He also said:

Therefore whosoever heareth these sayings of mine, and doeth them, I will liken him unto a wise man, which built his house upon a rock:

And the rain descended, and the floods came, and the winds blew, and beat upon that house; and it fell not: for it was founded upon a rock.

And every man that heareth these sayings of mine, and doeth them not, shall be likened unto a foolish man, which built his house upon the sand:

Faith That Makes a Demand on the Anointing

And the rain descended, and the floods came, and the winds blew, and beat upon that house; and it fell: and great was the fall of it.

MATTHEW 7:24-27

How the Devil Tries To Steal Your Faith

There are three areas where the devil will come in to try to steal your faith. You may be shocked at what they are — or maybe you won't be.

Number one is through *loved ones.*

Number two is through *religious leaders.* Even people who are supposed to be Full Gospel.

Number three, in Jesus' case, was through *His staff!* Ministers, if your staff members are not hooked up with your vision, they can talk you out of what God has for you.

Then after that saith he to his disciples [His staff], Let us go into Judaea again.

JOHN 11:7

Notice the word "go." *Faith will always go toward the miracle.* Faith never says, "When it comes to me, then I'll believe it. When it comes to me, it has really happened." You always go toward the miracle when you have faith.

As soon as he plants the seed, the farmer starts getting ready for the harvest. My father-in-law is a farmer, and after he plants his seed for a cotton crop, he gets his strippers and combines oiled up, because he knows he's going to get a harvest.

Act Like Your Miracle Is So

When you plant faith with your mouth for whatever you're believing God for, go as far as you can in the natural toward that miracle. *Act like you've already got it!*

If you're in a wheelchair, start buying some new clothes and shoes, and start thinking about what kind of sports activity you're going to get involved in. Go to the local ski shop and say, "I'm going skiing."

Why? Because *faith is always on the go.*

Notice what Jesus' disciples (staff) said:

His disciples say unto him, Master, the Jews of late sought to stone thee; and goest thou thither again?

JOHN 11:8

Faith Will Produce Every Time

What a staff! Now notice what came out of Jesus' mouth as He talked about walking in the light of this:

Are there not twelve hours in the day? If any man walk in the day, he stumbleth not, because he seeth the light of this world.

But if a man walk in the night, he stumbleth, because there is no light in him.

These things saith he: and after that he saith unto them, Our friend Lazarus sleepeth; but I go....

JOHN 11:9-11

Going Toward the Miracle

Again, faith will always *go* toward the miracle. Jesus finished His thought in verse 11 by saying, "Our friend Lazarus sleepeth; but I go, that I may awake him out of sleep." His staff is really going to get excited about this!

Then said his disciples, Lord, if he sleep he shall do well.

Howbeit Jesus spake of his death: but they thought that he had spoken of taking a rest in sleep.

Then said Jesus unto them plainly, Lazarus is dead.

JOHN 11:12-14

Sometimes you've just got to be plain. I don't like "religious" talk. I don't know why it is, but when people go into a church building sometimes — especially one with stained-glass windows — their voices change. They begin to talk "religiously."

I have a teaching about that called *"What Is a Humble Man?"* The Bible says, "Humble yourselves under the mighty hand of God, that he may exalt you in due time" (1 Peter 5:6).

I was shocked when the Holy Spirit began teaching me what a humble man really is. *A humble man is a man who will say what God says!* A humble man is a man who will take counsel from another person.

An egotist, on the other hand, won't take anyone else's word but his own.

When you talk God's Word, you are a humble man in the world, even though religious people may say you're being arrogant and egotistical.

Then said Jesus unto them plainly, Lazarus is dead.

Faith That Makes a Demand on the Anointing

> *And I am glad for your sakes that I was not there, to the intent ye may believe; nevertheless let us go unto him.*
>
> JOHN 11:14,15

There's that word "go" again.

Doubting Thomas Speaks Up

> *Then said Thomas [one of His staff members] ...unto his fellow disciples, Let us also go....*
>
> JOHN 11:16

Boy, that sounds positive. Have you ever been around religious people? "Oh, yes, let's go with Him."

But notice what Thomas added: "...that we may die with him." What a staff! They didn't have much faith in Jesus, did they? Praise God, later on they got full of the Holy Spirit. Well, let's go on. It gets worse.

> *Then when Jesus came, he found that he [Lazarus] had lain in the grave four days already.*
>
> JOHN 11:17

This isn't a warm body, my brother and sister — this is a *dead* one. He's already been dead four days!

Now Bethany was nigh unto Jerusalem, about fifteen furlongs off [about two miles]:

> *And many of the Jews came to Martha and Mary to comfort them concerning their brother.*
>
> JOHN 11:18,19

Religion Is Drawn to Death

Here come the religious leaders. It's amazing. God once told me, *"Religion is always drawn to death."*

Have you ever been to a funeral and encountered the religious relatives? When you get up to talk about Jesus and about them getting saved, they get mad. But if you get "religious" and cry and say something pious like, "The Lord giveth, and the Lord taketh away," they'll all get religious with you, and say, "Amen."

But if you say, "Bless God, she's not in there. She's in heaven, glory be to God, and we have come to this funeral to praise God that she's with Jesus," watch all the religious leaders. "My God,"

Faith Will Produce Every Time

they'll exclaim in horror, "that preacher is disrespectful of the dead!"

The devil doesn't like this kind of sermon. He's got to get that seed out of our hearts, just as he wanted to get it out of Jesus.

So he decided, "I've got to get one of these workers around Him to talk Him out of that. He can't go over there to Lazarus' tomb. That seed in Him will produce! "He was trying to get that seed.

You've got to watch out for deacons. Don't get mad at me, deacons, but you're not the pastor. Deacons are to serve, not to pastor.

I go to some churches, and the pastor can't do anything unless he asks the deacons' permission first. I once preached in a denominational church where the pastor was filled with the Holy Spirit. He was so excited about the meeting we were having! People were getting healed. Then the deacons fired him and kicked us out.

Within six months, five of them dropped dead, because God was moving in that church. They weren't resisting the pastor, as they thought, but God, and the devil had an open door into their lives to destroy them. When deacons make these kinds of decisions, it isn't proper church government anyway.

Don't Get Talked Out of Your Miracle

> *And many of the Jews came to Martha and Mary, to comfort them concerning their brother.*
>
> *Then Martha, as soon as she heard that Jesus was coming, went and met him: but Mary sat still in the house.*
>
> *Then said Martha unto Jesus,* **Lord, I'm glad you are here. Now we're going to have victory.**
>
> JOHN 11:19-21

Huh? No, that's not what she said. The devil already had tried to get the seed out of Jesus through the Mount of Temptation experience, and he failed, so he said, "I know I can't get it through Him — I've already tried that — so I'll get other people to talk Him out of that seed."

You might not like it, but the devil does use people to talk you out of your faith. He'll even use Full Gospel people if they will let him.

Faith That Makes a Demand on the Anointing

I didn't have trouble with the devil when one of the people in my church had a stroke; I had trouble with the Full Gospel folks. They were more concerned in trying to argue over a doctrinal difference. But I don't call their unbelief a doctrinal difference; I call it thinking the devil's thoughts.

I told them, "You're ganging up with the devil." (It makes religious people real mad when you tell them they're ganging up with the devil!)

Jesus said He loved Martha. Notice what she really said in verse 21:

> *Lord, if thou hadst been here, my brother had not died.*
>
> *But I know, that even now, whatsoever thou wilt ask of God, God will give it thee.*
>
> *Jesus said unto her, Thy brother shall rise again.*
>
> JOHN 11:21-23

Notice she said, "Lord, if thou *hadst* been here, my brother had not *died.*" The devil will always put it in the *past* or *future* tenses, but how about *now?* "Now faith is," the Bible says. How about right now? How about your miracle today? Not tomorrow, and not in the past, but how about right now, glory to God.

It should have been enough for Martha to hear Jesus say, "Thy brother shall rise again." But Martha replied:

> *I know that he shall rise again in the resurrection at the last day.*
>
> JOHN 11:24

Martha Turns Religious

That isn't what He meant, honey. You can try to help people like Martha, but don't let their unbelief rub off on you.

> *Jesus said unto her, I am the resurrection, and the life: he that believeth in me, though he were dead, yet shall he live:*
>
> *And whosoever liveth and believeth in me shall never die. Believest thou this?*
>
> JOHN 11:25,26

Doesn't that do something to you? Glory to God! But Martha got "religious" on Him.

Faith Will Produce Every Time

She saith unto him, Yea, Lord: I believe that thou art the Christ, the Son of God, which should come into the world.

And when she had so said, she went her way....

JOHN 11:27,28

Chapter 6

THE IMPORTANCE OF SAYING THE WORD

I'm going to tell you something, preachers: People want to hear the Word of God. They don't want to hear what you *think* about the situation. You must give your people the Word of God!

I know it's hard to be blunt, but you can be sweet and blunt at the same time.

After you give your loved ones the Word of God, sometimes the devil will bring someone else on the scene. This happened to the woman in my church who'd had the stroke. Her father got his pastor to come to the hospital. They said nothing about the Word of God or divine healing to her; all they talked about was politics while the doctors said there was no hope for her to live.

But her husband came into that hospital room, kicked out his father-in-law and his pastor, and started confessing the healing Word over her. And she's alive today because her husband was bold with the Word and bold against unbelief.

Guilt Trips

> And when she had so said, she went her way, and called Mary her sister secretly, saying, The Master is come, and calleth for thee.
> JOHN 11:28

This is no record of Jesus calling for Mary in the scriptures. Jesus never said it.

As soon as she heard that, she arose quickly, and came unto him.

Faith That Makes a Demand on the Anointing

Now Jesus was not come into the town, but was in that place where Martha met him.

> *The Jews then which were with her in the house, and comforted her, when they saw Mary, that she rose up hastily and went out, followed her, saying, She goeth unto the grave to weep there.*
>
> *Then when Mary was come where Jesus was, and saw him, she fell down at his feet, saying unto him, Lord, if thou hadst been here, my brother had not died.*
>
> LUKE 11:29-32

Note that word "if." *Guilt!* Have people ever tried to put you on a guilt trip? Have they said, "If you weren't out of town, that person wouldn't have died." Or, "If you were at the right place and listening to God, this would never have happened to me." Guilt, guilt, guilt!

People may try to put a pastor on a guilt trip by saying, "If you were doing your job, my kids wouldn't be out there on dope." Is that so?

How Parents Fail

Mom was at home watching "As the Stomach Turns" and daydreaming over some macho movie star instead of taking her kids to the youth group and encouraging them to get involved. And dad was off with his buddies playing sports or hanging out in some bar instead of being on his face before God, finding out what his children should do in life and then bringing them up in the ways of the Lord.

You may say, "I don't like that. That puts it back on me."

You've got it right: That puts the responsibility back on you. It isn't your pastor's responsibility for you to live the Christian life. His responsibility is to break the bread; to give out the Word. What you do with it is your responsibility.

Remember what Jesus said? "Therefore whosoever *heareth* these sayings of mine, and *doeth* them, I will liken him unto a wise man..." (Matthew 7:24). Many people have been attending good churches for four or five years, but they still don't go out and *do* God's Word — and you can't make them.

The Importance of Saying the Word
When the Devil Gets Worried

The devil says, "I've got to get that seed out of them. That seed is going to produce." However, the devil can't touch it. No one can touch it but you. Once you plant it out of your mouth, you're the only one who can dig it up.

We have had thousands of people go through our church in 13 1/2 years of pastoring. Pastors, how many have you had go through your church? You've had a lot, haven't you? You just don't want to admit it.

Why don't they stay? As you preach the Word, they shout, "Bless God, I believe it that way. I'm going to go out and do it." And when they start doing it, the devil comes and tries to steal that seed. So they get discouraged, because they thought they had found a free ticket to the easy life. They didn't really realize that this life of faith would be opposed by the devil.

One woman told me, "Bless God, I had hardly any problems until I came to your church. I'm going back to my religious church!"

I explained, "When you came over here, you became a target for the devil, because he's going to try to get that Word out of you."

He'll try to use relatives and friends of yours to steal it. They'll say, "Now, don't get into that *extreme* bunch." Extreme *what?* Extreme believing in the Word?

They'll say, "Don't get hooked up with that hyper faith bunch." Well, blind Bartimaeus was sure hyper on faith, and he got *his* miracle! Religious devils don't like this kind of preaching.

...Lord, if thou hadst been here, my brother had not died.

When Jesus therefore saw her weeping, and the Jews also weeping which came with her, he groaned in the spirit, and was troubled.

And said, Where have ye laid him? They said unto him, Lord, come and see.

Jesus wept.

JOHN 11:32-35

Jesus wasn't crying because Lazarus was dead. In Sunday School they used to tell us that. I know that's the shortest verse in

Faith That Makes a Demand on the Anointing

the New Testament, but Jesus wasn't weeping because Lazarus was dead. *He was weeping because of their unbelief!"*

Then said the Jews, Behold how he loved him!

JOHN 11:36

Here came the religious leaders to add their two cents' worth. Isn't that sweet? But notice what they said out of the *other* side of their mouths: "Could not this man, being a faith man, hooked up with that hyper faith bunch, which opened the eyes of the blind, have caused that even this man should not have died?" (my paraphrase of verse 37).

What About Tragedy?

I've had religious people tell me such things at times when the devil has put tragedies in my path. They have said, "What has happened to you *now*, big faith man? I know someone who believed that way and died."

Well, I'd rather die in faith than in unbelief! I don't understand why people don't think it's a *victory* when people go on to be with Jesus. I'd rather be with Jesus than anything.

We get so earthly minded, we forget there's another world out there. If you could just see into that other realm — if God would open your eyes right now — you would see some of your loved ones who went home to be with the Lord. And they aren't just lying around playing harps, either. They're involved with us, for we are encompassed about with "so great a cloud of witnesses," according to Hebrews 12:1. Glory be to God!

Just minutes before she died, my mother gave her heart to Jesus. She had been an alcoholic all her life. Then — *boom* — she left this world. She's up in heaven now, learning about faith in Smith Wigglesworth's class.

If you don't learn about faith down here, you're going to have to learn about it when you get up there, because that's how you're going to function — by faith.

Another Real World

There's another real world out there, so don't fall apart if someone dies. If he or she was saved, walk into the funeral parlor praising God.

The Importance of Saying the Word

That body of theirs was just their "shell." It was their "Earth suit." All it does is give you permission to be on this Earth. That's why Jesus had to have an Earth suit, too. That's why He had to come through a woman's womb. Did any of you come any other way? When you've got an Earth suit on, it gives you a legal right to be on this Earth.

The real you, on the inside of that Earth suit, is your spirit. You will never die.

Jesus therefore again groaning in himself cometh to the grave. It was a cave, and a stone lay upon it.

Jesus said, Take ye away the stone.

JOHN 11:38,39

The devil was still saying, "I've got to get that seed. What am I going to do now? He's saying 'Take away the stone!' He's going toward the miracle! I'll put another loved one beside Him."

...Martha, the sister of him that was dead, saith unto him, Lord, by this time he stinketh, for he hath been dead four days.

Jesus said unto her, Said I not unto thee, that, if thou wouldest believe, thou shouldest see the glory of God?

JOHN 11:39,40

Strength in Unity

How many of you want to see the glory of God show up in your church?

Remember back in Genesis, when the people were trying to build that Tower of Babel? God came down and said:

Behold, the people is one, and they have all one language; and this they begin to do: and now nothing will be restrained from them, which they have imagined to do.

Go to, let us go down, and there confound their language, that they may not understand one another's speech.

So the Lord scattered them abroad from thence upon the face of all the earth: and they left off to build the city.

GENESIS 11:6-8

Why did God confuse their language? There was a principle involved: They were all saying the same thing! God said, "Nothing

Faith That Makes a Demand on the Anointing

will be restrained from them, which they have imagined to do."

That word "imagine" in the Hebrew means, "Whatever they 'design' to do will not be restrained from them." What does this mean? It refers to whatever you design in your spirit.

Pastor, that new building you see in your spirit won't be restrained from you as long as you talk about it! Don't tell too many people about it, though, or they'll talk you out of it, saying, "Rough times are ahead. Be careful!" (That's why I never have a vote on what color carpet we should put in the church. We'd have a fight over it.)

"Nothing will be restrained...." That's the way Jesus operates. He was keeping His words in line with the Word of God. He was saying what the Word says, and it could not be restrained. When you do this, the glory will show up for you, too.

Why did God say nothing would be restrained from those building the tower? Because all the people were saying the same thing!

Unless your staff members share your vision and say what you are saying, you'll never fulfill your God-given vision. That's why it is important for pastors to get their congregations saying the same thing, too.

What is the vision of your church? Is it to change your city for God? Of course, there are other churches in your city, and if they share the vision, you all need to say the same thing. It won't be restrained: God will move in your city!

Chapter 7

WHEN THE GLORY SHOWS UP

God wants to manifest His glory in your church, but every department must enhance and not hinder the move of the Spirit. That's why music is so important in churches — the right kind of music with an anointing on it. If it's right, the glory cloud will come in.

I've never seen the devil fight so many music groups. A musician will get mad and say, "Bless God, I didn't get a chance to sing or play tonight."

"Well, the Holy Ghost moved a different way."

"I don't care! I want my way. I'm quitting."

You know I'm speaking the truth.

That's why the devil was sending different people to Jesus. He hoped Jesus would change His words about raising Lazarus from the dead, because he knew Jesus was the only one who could dig that seed up and stop this miracle from happening.

Isn't that something? And you're the only one who can stop *your* miracle. If it is stopped, we usually blame it all on the devil. We say, "I didn't get my miracle. The devil did it." No, *you* did it.

You give more credit to the devil than he deserves. He has no power. He has been stripped of his power, and can't hurt you. He doesn't have any teeth! All he can do is "gum" you. He just yells and tries to scare you from acting in faith.

God told the devil back in Genesis 3:15, "I am going to get you! The One who comes out of the woman's womb is going to bruise your head, and you are going to bruise His heel." Those

Faith That Makes a Demand on the Anointing

bruises were laid on Jesus at Calvary, and He defeated the devil for you and me!

Martha's Warning

> *The devil said to himself, "I've got to throw one more shot."* And Martha said, *"By this time, Lord, he stinketh."* As if that's going to stop God!
>
> *Then they took away the stone from the place where the dead was laid. And Jesus lifted up his eyes and said, Father....*
>
> JOHN 11:41

This is one of my favorite verses of scripture. When it gets right down to it, He isn't only God; He's *Father.*

> *...Father, I thank thee that thou hast heard me.*
>
> JOHN 11:41

When did God hear Him? *Four days before, when He planted the seed.* Four days before, when He said, "He will live and not die." That's when God heard Him. What faith!

What Is Faith?

Once I said, "God, we hear a lot of definitions of faith. What is faith?"

He said, *"Faith is walking in fellowship with Me."* When you know God, you won't doubt Him. When you walk in fellowship with God, you'll know what faith is. Believe in Him. If He said it, you'll believe it, and that will settle it.

We've all heard that saying, "God said it, I believe it, and that settles it." Well, you can leave out the middle phrase. God said it and that settles it, whether you believe it or not. In other words, if God already said it, that settles it. I choose to believe it.

Jesus always honors faith. Never put down faith teachers. Just because they are preaching on faith and some people go out and goof up doesn't mean the teaching isn't true. Just because they preach on prosperity and some people do all kinds of goofy things doesn't mean it's not true. Don't throw the baby out with the bath water.

The Seed Produces

> ...*Father, I thank thee that thou hast heard me.*
>
> *That seed is about ready to produce!*
>
> *And I knew that thou hearest me always: but because of the people which stand by I said it, that they may believe that thou hast sent me.*
>
> *And when he thus had spoken, he cried with a loud voice, Lazarus, come forth.*
>
> JOHN 11:41-43

It's a good thing Jesus called forth Lazarus by name; otherwise, a lot of dead people would have come out of their graves!

> *And he that was dead came forth, bound hand and foot with graveclothes: and his face was bound about with a napkin. Jesus said unto them, Loose him, and let him go.*
>
> JOHN 11:44

That seed produced the glory — the resurrection power that pulled the dead man out of his grave.

What Happened at Lazarus' Tomb

Today you can visit what is supposed to be Lazarus' tomb in Bethany. If it is the original tomb, there is a round hole in the ground where his body was supposedly laid.

Have you ever wondered how Lazarus got out of there? That's how my mind thinks. I asked, "Lord, how did You get Lazarus out of there?" He was bound in graveclothes that were like a hard body cast, and the Bible doesn't say anyone went down and pulled him up out of there.

Then God said, *"The glory."*

It was the resurrection power! Lazarus got *blasted* out of that cave and shot out the mouth of it to where Jesus stood. And Jesus said, "Loose him, and let him go!"

God said, "You tell my people that I'm no respecter of persons, and what I did for Jesus, I'll do for them. Your miracle will show up the same way." Glory be to God!

Faith That Makes a Demand on the Anointing

You Can Have What You Say

Jesus did it with His mouth: He planted that miracle with His mouth. Did you see that? *You can have what you say!* If you don't like what you have around you, change your mouth.

This is powerful stuff! No wonder blind Bartimaeus wouldn't shut up, even though Jesus' disciples probably went around with the others, telling people, "Oh, He's holy. Don't bother Him. Shhh!"

Jesus said, "Lazarus will live and not die." That's the seed He planted. The devil said, "I've got to get that seed!" He tried to do it through influencing loved ones, religious leaders, and the people Jesus worked with — the same three methods he still uses today.

The Lord told me it is especially important to have the right staff. We also need to check ourselves to make sure we're all saying what our pastor is saying, because he is the leader of the church.

Jesus said what the Word said, and every time you say what the Word says, the devil will send people to get you off that track.

Handling Criticism

If the devil appeared to any of us, I think most of us would know how to handle him. We would know to say, "Get out of here in the Name of Jesus!" But it's hard to handle people, and it's hard to handle their criticism.

Don't you want to be loved? I want to be loved by everyone. If you are a pastor, sometimes you get word back that So-and-so left the church because you said something that offended him. That hurts you, doesn't it?

That's why my staff keeps bad letters away from me. They throw them in the trash can to protect my spirit. You need to protect your pastor in these ways, too.

If someone gets offended and leaves, just "plant" him, and get a hundredfold return — not of his attitude, but a hundred people back.

Buckets of Money

The devil tried to attack our finances one Christmastime. A

powerful evangelist who attended the church got up in the New Year's Eve service and raised more than $4,000 for our ministry so we could pay some debts we had. Both of us had just had meetings cancelled at the last minute, which created a financial hardship.

He told me later that he put his last $100 in the offering. I didn't know he had put that money in, but God did. I was moving in the Spirit and didn't know what he had done. At the end of the service, God said, "Call the guest minister up here." I prophesied over him, he fell under the power, and God said, "Fire on his feet. Fire — an evangelist on fire! Put a bucket by each foot." The ushers put buckets by each foot.

I said, "God told me this man needs a miracle. Everyone who puts some money in those buckets is going to have part of his reward." The people ran up there, quickly filling those buckets with money.

The minister told me later, "I gave my last $100. I didn't have a place to preach for two more weeks, and we didn't have any food or anything." God met his need instantly. Because he planted that seed, the glory showed up for him.

How many of you want the glory to show up for you? I'll tell you, pastors: If you get your congregation and staff all saying the same thing and sharing the same vision, your vision will not be restrained. God will help you affect your city, and the glory will show up in your church. (But sometimes it takes a cleaning out to do it.)

Defeated in Finances?

Do you know how the devil defeats many Christians in the area of money? He talks them out of paying tithes and offerings. He says, "Oh, don't give. You mean you're going to give in three offerings today? Oh no, don't do that."

If you don't plant money, you won't get money back. If you plant corn, you get corn. That's just the way it works. It's one of God's laws, like the law of gravity.

I just showed you out of the Word of God how the glory will show up every time for you. The only one who can stop your miracle is you.

Chapter 8

UNDERSTANDING THE PROPHET'S MANTLE

> *And it shall come to pass in that day, that his burden shall be taken away from off thy shoulder, and his yoke from off thy neck, and the yoke shall be destroyed because of the anointing.*
>
> ISAIAH 10:27

We need the anointing of God in our churches today to destroy the yokes and the burdens that get on people.

The fourth chapter of Second Kings tells about the widow of one of the sons of the prophets who was about to be crushed by such a yoke.

As you know, Elisha, the prophet of God blessed her, instructing her to gather empty pots. God filled them all with oil, and she paid all her bills! The seventh verse says:

> *Then she came and told the man of God. And he said, Go, sell the oil, and pay thy debt, and live thou and thy children of the rest.*

Today people are so much in debt, they've almost got their kids listed as collateral. That is as bad as what was happening in ancient Israel, where the widow's creditors wanted to take her children for bondmen when she couldn't pay the family's debts.

Until now, we haven't really seen the working of miracles in its fullest capacity. But in this day and age we are going to see the working of miracles in a powerful way. Things are going to be *multiplied!* Your money, like that oil, is going to be multiplied.

Faith That Makes a Demand on the Anointing

The Woman Who Blessed a Prophet

The ninth verse tells about another woman, the Shumammite woman, who blessed the prophet Elisha:

And she said unto her husband, Behold now, I perceive that this is an holy man of God, which passeth by us continually.

Men of God may pass through your town, but you don't always bless them. Many of you see your pastor all the time — so much so that it's easy to take him for granted. You ought to take care of him.

You ought to show your pastor how much you love him, and it ought to go beyond a mere pat on the back. That gesture doesn't last very long, as you husbands know. You'd better bring that wife of yours some flowers and gifts once in a while as well as telling her you love her and giving her a hurried peck on the cheek.

Even a lot of tithers are not blessed because they don't take care of their preachers very well. Preachers, it's time that God blessed you! When your congregation wants to give you a new car or some other gift, accept it gracefully.

The Royal Treatment

The Shunammite woman continued (verse 10):

Let us make a little chamber, I pray thee, on the wall; and let us set for him there a bed, and a table, and a stool, and a candlestick: and it shall be, when he cometh to us, that he shall turn in thither.

If you will study this, you will find this wasn't just any old room; it was built on the front of the house over the porch. It wasn't furnished cheaply, either. That stool was really like a throne.

> And it fell on a day, that he came thither, and he turned into the chamber, and lay there.
>
> And he said to Gehazi his servant, Call this Shunammite. And when he had called her, she stood before him.
>
> And he said unto him, Say now unto her, Behold, thou hast been careful for us with all this care....
>
> 2 KINGS 4:11-13

You ought to be careful how you treat a man of God. This

Understanding the Prophet's Mantle

woman and her household were very careful to make sure that Elisha and his servant were blessed. That old saying, "Lord, You keep the preacher humble, and we'll keep him poor" is not God's prayer; it a stingy deacon's prayer!

"What Is To Be Done for Thee?"

> ...*what is to be done for thee? wouldest thou be spoken for to the king, or to the captain of the host?*
>
> *And she answered, I dwell among mine own people.*
>
> *And he said, What then is to be done for her? and Gehazi answered, Verily she hath no child, and her husband is old.*
>
> 2 KINGS 4:13,14

What was Gehazi saying? The woman was much younger than her husband, and he could not father a child.

> *And he said, Call her. And when he had called her, she stood in the door.*
>
> *And he said, About this season, according to the time of life, thou shalt embrace a son. And she said, Nay, my lord, thou man of God, do not lie unto thine handmaiden.*
>
> 2 KINGS 4:15,16

The prophet was proclaiming a blessing over the couple. Prophets can do this. You'd better watch out around a prophet's ministry. Time after time, people have written me, reporting that barren women came to one of our meetings, were under the influence of the prophet's anointing, and several months later conceived and then had children.

No one prayed for them, and they didn't know they were healed in their wombs. Yet time revealed that they had been healed.

The Blessing Arrives

> *And the woman conceived, and bare a son at that season that Elisha had said unto her, according to the time of life.*
>
> *And when the child was grown, it fell on a day, that he went out to his father to the reapers.*
>
> *And he said unto his father, My head, my head. And he said to a lad, Carry him to his mother.*
>
> 2 KINGS 4:17-19

This was obviously a sunstroke.

And when he had taken him, and brought him to his mother, he sat on her knees till noon, and then died.

2 KINGS 4:20

Here it is, perhaps 16 to 18 years later, and the promised son died! However, people back then understood the prophet's anointing. People today don't understand anything about the mantle that is on the prophet.

The Pastor's Mantle

As a matter of fact, they don't even understand the mantle that is on the pastor! If they understood the mantle that is on the pastor, they wouldn't talk about him or treat him the way they do.

In the eleventh through the thirteenth chapters of First Corinthians, Paul is talking about discerning the Lord's Body. Where he says, "Now concerning spiritual gifts, brethren, I would not have you ignorant" (1 Corinthians 12:1), he is referring to the gifts, plural. Paul is talking about the gift ministries and the gifts of the Holy Spirit.

Learning What the Scriptures Say

We are going to have to learn to go by the Word of God, because God has established certain principles in there. I'm glad Paul said, "And God hath set some in the church..." (1 Corinthians 12:28). *God set. God set.* I'm glad that God set them, not men.

It is not scriptural for a deacon board to set a pastor in the church and then run the pastor. You can't find that in the Bible. That's a man-made rule. Usually you end up with a bunch of *carnal* men trying to run a *spiritual* man, and that isn't the way it is supposed to be!

My goodness, if this Shunammite woman discerned and knew the anointing that was on the prophet of God, how much more should we discern it today, when we have more light on the subject than people in ancient Israel had?

However, we are getting closer to the day when more revelation knowledge is going to be released about the gift ministries and the gifts of the Spirit.

Understanding the Prophet's Mantle

Many people are trying to walk in someone else's mantle, and that's why it never works for them. It just doesn't work! We must learn the calling that God anointed and marked us for, and we must walk in that.

Many of you are in the ministry of helps. Many of you businessmen are called to make money for God.

"Well, yeah, but I barely make it."

It's because you don't have it right according to the Word of God. As soon as God starts blessing a businessman and he starts giving to the church, the first thing he wants to do is control the pastor and the church.

"I gave the church $100,000 last year, and I don't want that kind of carpet in there."

You have no right to say that.

"Well, I gave my money!"

No, it isn't *your* money. It belongs to God. He just put the ministry of helps on you so you can make money for the Gospel.

A Mother's Faith

> *The Shumammite woman knew about the mantle that was on the man of God.*
>
> *And she went up, and laid him [her dead son] on the bed of the man of God, and shut the door upon him, and went out.*
>
> 2 KINGS 4:21

The prophet's anointing was *saturated* in those sheets and that bed!

> *And she called unto her husband, and said, Send me, I pray thee, one of the young men, and one of the asses....*
>
> 2 KINGS 4:22

She's a submitted woman, isn't she? Back then, her donkey was like a Cadillac today. She had some money. She explained to her husband,

> *...that I may run to the man of God, and come again.*
>
> *And he said, Wherefore wilt thou go to him to day? it is neither new moon, nor sabbath. And she said, It shall be well.*
>
> 2 KINGS 4:22,23

Notice she didn't say anything about their dead child.

Faith That Makes a Demand on the Anointing

A Desperate Journey

> *Then she saddled an ass, and said to her servant, Drive, and go forward; slack not thy riding for me, except I bid thee.*
>
> 2 KINGS 4:24

In modern terms, she was saying, "Put the metal to the pedal. I don't care if it's 65 miles an hour — hit it, man! We've got to get to the man of God! I don't care if we hit a sandstorm or a snowstorm on the way. And don't stop because I'm a woman; don't stop for anything unless I tell you to."

> *So she went and came unto the man of God to mount Carmel.*
>
> 2 KINGS 4:25

That's quite a mountain! I've seen it. If the woman was down in that valley, it must have taken her quite a while to get to the top of the mountain.

> *And it came to pass, when the man of God saw her afar off, that he said to Gehazi his servant, Behold, yonder is that Shumammite:*
>
> *Run now, I pray thee, to meet her, and say unto her, Is it well with thee? is it well with thy husband? is it well with the child? And she answered, It is well.*
>
> 2 KINGS 4:25,26

A Good Confession

She had a good confession. She didn't say, "O man of God, You gave me this prophecy, and I had the child, and now you let me down!" That's what some people do. They get mad at the man of God. They get mad at the pastor. They get mad at the teacher.

Honey, your problem isn't your pastor, the teacher, or God. Most of the time it's you. It is you who have to make the correction.

"Well, my pastor... If he only..."

Instead of reading your Sunday paper on Sunday morning and coming to church dry as a cob, expecting your pastor to be on fire for God, why don't you spend an hour in prayer before you come to church? Then watch what will happen.

> *And when she came to the man of God to the hill, she caught him by the feet: but Gehazi came near to thrust her away. And the man of God said, Let her alone....*
>
> 2 KINGS 4:27

Understanding the Prophet's Mantle

Notice how much she knew about the mantle that was on the prophet of God. She was going to grab it. Doesn't that remind you of blind Bartimaeus? You've got to understand this is the way people in Bible days looked at things: They looked at a prophet of God differently from the way we do.

We think the prophet of God lives in a cave, has a beard, hasn't taken a bath in 30 days, and stinks. Just because someone gets up and prophesies, he thinks he's a prophet. That isn't a prophet.

The gift of prophecy is a gift from the Holy Spirit. The prophet can have the gift of prophecy in operation, but the prophet's anointing goes deeper than that. A prophet goes into the spirit realm and deals with things in the spirit that only "spiritual generals" deal with.

There's Something About a Prophet

There's something about a prophet: When he goes into the spirit, he doesn't necessarily have to do it in a meeting in front of other people; he can deal with spiritual forces alone in prayer.

I've been in cities where I would go into the spirit, and I would see the spirit that was over that city. I would deal with that spirit, and I would see it fall. After I'd left town, the pastor would report, "There was a complete turnabout in our church after you left."

A preacher friend of mine calls me a "tide-changer." I didn't understand what he meant at first. One day I got in prayer and said, "God, what does that mean? People have been calling me a tide-changer when I go in their church. When we flow with the Spirit of God, things will change in our churches."

The ministry of a prophet deals with things that go on in the spirit. It doesn't mean he's more spiritual than any other Christian; it's because of the mantle that he goes deeper and is keener in the spirit and sees things.

"What Do You See?"

God asked Jeremiah, "What is it that you *see?*"

He replied, "I see an almond tree." What is an almond tree? An almond tree blossoms before any other tree in Israel. An almond tree, therefore, is like a rooster that crows before anyone else gets up.

Faith That Makes a Demand on the Anointing

Then what was God saying? He was showing Jeremiah that he was a prophet of God and that He reveals things to His prophets before other people find out about them.

The Bible says, "If you listen to the prophets — true prophets, not flakes — you will prosper" (2 Chronicles 20:20). Prophets just have a deeper, keener anointing.

I've been in meetings where Brother Kenneth E. Hagin dealt with spirits affecting the political scene three years before anything happened. That's why we must pray for the prophet's ministry to come on the scene in meetings. Prophets can deal with the most powerful spirits in the spirit realm.

The Way the Prophet Operates

I cannot turn the gift on or off. If I could, I would operate in it as much as possible. But it is as the Spirit wills — and *the people must create an atmosphere for the prophet to minister*. That is why I must pray over every invitation I receive and make sure the pastor understands the way I flow.

Some people say, "We want you to come to our church, and this is what we want you to do. Oh, no, we don't want you to bring anyone. We've got our own music."

I have to tell them, "That's fine, but the Lord told me that if I'm to come, I've got to bring a particular musician with me. Your musicians can help us, but when I'm ministering and I get in the spirit, I must have exactly the right song, and a musician I'm familiar with understands that. That's the way God moves with me."

If the pastor won't agree, I won't go to his church. Is it because I think I'm a big shot? No, I'm not trying to be a big shot; I'm just saying that we cannot play games anymore.

Everyone is trying to be a jack-of-all-trades, and it isn't working. When someone tries to walk in another person's mantle, it could kill him. Some people even die prematurely when they do this.

We're under grace now, and it takes a little longer for you to die, but in the Old Testament if you walked into the Holy of Holies and you weren't wearing the mantle of the High Priest, you dropped deader than a doornail.

Understanding the Prophet's Mantle

In fact, they used to tie a rope around the High Priest when he entered the Holy of Holies once a year, and if it got too quiet in there, and they no longer could hear the pomegranate decorations tinkling on his robe, they would pull his dead body out. It meant he had been struck dead because he had sin in his life.

It's very, very important that we walk in our own anointing!

Chapter 9

MAKING A DEMAND ON THE PROPHET'S ANOINTING

The full measure of Jesus' ministry is distributed throughout the whole Body of Christ. That's why He said, corporately speaking, *"...lay hands on the sick, and they shall recover"* (Mark 16:18).

How many of you have ever laid hands on the sick and felt a tingling or a warmth come out of your hands? You made contact with the anointing that is on the whole Body of Christ.

The prophet's anointing is a different, deeper anointing. Jesus went around and said He was anointed. Today's ministries, too, need to tell the people they are anointed. The reason we back off is because we are afraid we are going to take God's glory. And we should be mindful of that, because we shouldn't take any glory that belongs to God.

Also, because we don't want anyone looking to man for healing, we have completely backed off and gone in the opposite direction: We won't say anything about the anointing that is on us prophets.

However, if we would teach the people that it isn't the man who heals them — it is the *mantle* on his life — it would be a different story.

I have been very careful in presenting this truth that God has revealed to me through the years, yet I wouldn't say anything about being a prophet. I knew it would attract "kooks" to my meetings. Eventually, however, I came to realize we're always

Faith That Makes a Demand on the Anointing

going to have "kooks," and we shouldn't stop the plan of God because of them.

Now let's see how Elisha operated.

The Demand on Elisha's Mantle

Then he returned, and walked in the house to and fro....

2 KINGS 4:35

I'm glad I found someone else who walks and prays at the same time!

...and went up, and stretched himself upon him: and the child sneezed seven times, and the child opened his eyes.

And he called Gehazi, and said, call this Shunammite. So he called her. And when she was come in unto him, he said, Take up thy son.

Then she went in, and fell at his feet, and bowed herself to the ground, and took up her son, and went out.

2 KINGS 4:35-37

The child would never have been raised up unless the mother's faith was involved and made a demand on that mantle. Once she reached the prophet Elisha on Mount Carmel, she caught him by the feet and vowed she would not leave him. At first he didn't understand her actions, and Gehazi tried to pull her off.

Then finding out the child had died, the prophet sent Gehazi hurrying ahead to the woman's home to place his staff on the child, but Gehazi couldn't raise the dead child.

The Prophet's Reward

The Bible says, *"When you receive a prophet in the name of a prophet, you receive a prophet's reward"* (Matthew 10:41). This Shunammite mother received the prophet's reward when her child was restored to her.

Remember, she didn't ask for money or social position from the prophet when he had wanted to bless her years before. She needed neither money nor introductions to high society. She said, "I'm high society myself; I already know all those people."

Then Elisha's servant reminded the prophet that she and her husband were childless because her husband was old. God rejuvenated the husband, and she conceived and bore a child.

Making a Demand on the Prophet's Anointing

When her son died in his early teens, the Shunammite knew about a prophet's reward. She went to that prophet and drew again on his mantle in her time of distress.

Making a Demand on the Reward

Everyone who invests in a prophet's ministry invests in the mantle on the prophet's life. Therefore, *everyone who invests has a right to make a demand on that mantle when he or she needs a miracle like this — a prophet's miracle.*

The same thing happened to the widow of Zarephath who obeyed the prophet Elijah and made him a little cake of all the food left in her house (1 Kings 17). He blessed her, and her food was supernaturally replenished during a time of drought. You see, there's another way to get a miracle.

All of you have a right to make a demand on a prophet's reward when you invest in it. You don't have to believe this if you don't want to. I just share it with people, and then it's their business what they do with it.

I know the scripture, "Give and it shall be given to you," yet there also are rewards in the area of the ministry of a prophet. Prophets are friends of God. Prophets walk with God. They are keener in the Spirit than the other ministry gifts; it just goes along with their mantle. It doesn't mean they are superspiritual. It's all part of their mantle.

What Is a Mantle?

At times when I'm preaching, I use a pastor to illustrate what a mantle really is. I ask him to put his Bible down and remove his coat. Then I have an usher put his coat back on him. In the spirit realm, that is really what a mantle resembles: a coat.

When you step out of your body, you really just slip your "Earth coat" off and you slip on the mantle of your calling.

There are different kinds of mantles, and the Church needs every one of them. A true apostle has a tremendous mantle. A true New Testament evangelist has miracles, signs, and wonders following him.

The Anointing Drives Spirits Out

Because the Shunammite woman knew about the prophet's

Faith That Makes a Demand on the Anointing

mantle and how to make a demand on it, the prophet Elisha went into the chamber and lay on top of the child's dead body. His anointing overcame the spirit of death. You don't hear too much preaching on this. However, we can bring this same principle over into the New Testament. Acts 19:11,12 says:

And God wrought special miracles by the hands of Paul:

So that from his body were brought unto the sick handkerchiefs or aprons, and the diseases departed from them, and the evil spirits went out of them.

There's just something about a prophet of God: There's a tangible anointing on him. In fact, every prophet I've known has a strong tangible anointing. There are different degrees of anointings, and there are different anointings, but there is a tangible anointing on a prophet.

Paul was a prophet of God. (He was an apostle, but he also walked as a prophet.) When that anointing hit those cloths, it came off the prophet's mantle that was on Paul.

Delivered by the Anointing

Once when I was holding a meeting in Germany, people were getting healed all over the building. Suddenly, green foam started coming out of the mouth of a middle-aged woman who had fallen under the anointing of God. God told me that a spirit of infirmity had attached itself to her. She had been sickly all her life, but that anointing went into her and drove out everything that had been oppressing her.

God said, "I want to teach you something. Those are devils of sickness and disease that were passed down through her family from generation to generation."

She was always the first one to get a cold, and she always had it the longest. Those demons of sickness and disease were passed through the family, and the anointing was driving them out. She made an awful sound as they came out!

I always thought the way to cast out devils was by saying, "In the Name of Jesus, come out!" *But there is another way to cast out devils, and that's with the anointing!*

That's why, when a church has a strong anointing on it, people will either be saved, healed, and delivered just sitting there, or else they'll run out the back door and claim you are a false pastor or a false prophet. Devils can't stand that anointing. They go crazy when they're around it!

Once when I was preaching in Chicago, the power of God came in that place — there were about a thousand people there — and suddenly a woman stood up and started cussing me. I said, "Come out of her!" Boldness came on me, and I started running after her, chairs flying all over the place. She ran down the aisle and out the door.

The other woman who was with her lay down like a puppy dog and got delivered in the Name of Jesus. *The anointing destroys the yoke.*

Why Stay in a Dead Church?

I can't figure out why some of you who visit anointed churches go back to that old dead church of yours. You need hands laid on your head!

People have told me, "Well, you know, I've invested so much there, I've been there so long, and the Lord told me to stay there to help save it."

I've answered, "Honey, you'll sink with that thing. You can't go any higher than the pastor. If the pastor doesn't believe in it, you can't go beyond him. Get into a church where the Spirit is flowing. Get into a church where people dance in the Holy Ghost, where healings are taking place, and where they're casting out devils. Don't stay in that old dead church!

It may take some of you a little time to adjust to an anointed church. You will say at first, "O my God, I got in this church by accident!" No, you're in the *right* place.

The Woman Who Spent All She Had

In the light of this, the story of the woman with the issue of blood will be clearer to you.

> *And a certain woman, which had an issue of blood twelve years,*
>
> *And had suffered many things of many physicians, and had spent all that she had, and was nothing bettered, but rather grew worse....*
>
> MARK 5:25,26

Faith That Makes a Demand on the Anointing

This woman was once very wealthy, but she had spent all her money on doctors. God showed me that the medical industry is going to be furious with certain churches during this next wave. So many people will be going to these churches to be healed, they will empty the hospitals! That's right.

Some of you have made doctors millionaires. The other night on the late news there was a story about a little baby who was dying. Doctors have the equipment to save the baby's life, but it is tied up in a lawsuit because different doctors are fighting over royalties. Are they fighting to help humanity? No, they're fighting for money!

Don't misunderstand me — not all doctors are like that, and doctors have done a lot to help humanity, but the devil tries to get his hand of greed involved.

Look to a Healing Jesus!

It took this woman in the Bible 12 years to deplete all her money. Isn't it a shame she had to hit rock bottom before she looked to a healing Jesus? She spent all she had; those doctors took all her money. I guarantee, the reason she was out in the street was because she didn't have any money left.

We need to get back to a healing Jesus! We need to believe in Jesus. I am not stating that doctors are bad. They are fighting the same devil we are fighting. What I am stating is that we have put medical science *before* Jesus. But if we would fill our hearts and minds with the healing Word, we would find Jesus to be the greatest, most trustworthy physician.

We need to get back to discerning the Lord's Body. As we saw in First Corinthians 11:30, "For this cause many are weak and sickly among you, and many sleep."

We must also understand what Jesus did for us on Calvary, paying the price for our healing. There are different ways to receive healing. *That's how much God loves you!*

For example, there is healing through anointing with oil, prayer by church elders, prayer cloths, two persons agreeing in prayer, and receiving with your own faith without anyone else praying for you.

Making a Demand on the Prophet's Anointing

But we must not overlook the healing power that is manifested when that tangible healing anointing is imparted into the body of a sick person, and he receives it into his body by faith.

Discerning the Prophet's Anointing

The woman with the issue of blood discerned the prophet's anointing on *Jesus* just like the Shunammite woman had discerned the prophet's anointing on *Elisha*. This is what happened to her:

> *When she had heard of Jesus, [she] came in the press behind, and touched his garment.*
> MARK 5:27

Why did she do that? She knew Jesus was a prophet of God! Back then, people went to the prophet to get healing because many of the prophets during the time of the Old Testament were known to be anointed with healing power. Today you don't have to.

Today, there are different ways to receive healing, and one valid way is to have someone who is anointed with healing power lay hands on you and minister healing to you.

God anoints men to *heal* just like He anoints them to *preach*. He anointed Paul to heal — we just read about it. He anointed Jesus with healing power. It was in His mantle. That is what the woman with the issue of blood was drawn to.

She joined the crowd of people surrounding Jesus. Many of them touched Jesus that day, but they didn't release their faith while touching Him like she did.

Another translation of verse 27 says, "When she heard of Jesus, she came in the press behind, and touched His *mantle*." When I first read this, I thought back to the Old Testament prophets.

Why We Need Prophets Today

It has often been said during the teaching movement, "We are not led by a prophet's ministry today." That is true. Today we are led by the Holy Spirit. But how many people are keen in the Spirit and are listening to the leading of the Spirit?

Very few people are sensitive to the Holy Spirit. That is why we still need the prophets. They bring light on biblical truths on which the teachers can build a foundation.

Faith That Makes a Demand on the Anointing

There are still people among us who came out of the 1907 wave, yet they're spiritually dead — and they're in Full Gospel, Pentecostal denominations!

Some of these denominations have invested millions of dollars' worth of missionary money in the stock market instead of putting it in Gospel work, supporting missionaries, evangelists, and other workers with it.

Come Expecting a Miracle

For she said, If I may touch but his clothes, I shall be whole.
MARK 5:28

Do you remember the Shunammite woman who grabbed Elisha's feet and wouldn't let him go until she got her miracle? Do you remember that blind Bartimaeus' "begging" kind of faith really wasn't that of a beggar? There was a sense of persistence in it. When you come to Jesus with a great need, you must believe Him for the answer and go after your miracle until you see it. Don't give up, and don't let people talk you out of it.

And straightway the fountain of her blood was dried up; And she felt in her body that she was healed of that plague.

And Jesus, immediately knowing in himself that virtue had gone out of him, turned him about in the press, and said, Who touched my clothes [or mantle]?
MARK 5:29,30

He asked, "Who touched my clothes (or mantle)? Someone made a demand on my mantle — I *felt* it!"

The disciples replied, "There are people all around you. Why are You asking such a thing?"

"Because someone made a demand on Me."

Of course, many other people had touched Him, but they hadn't made a demand on His mantle with their faith.

The Real Jesus

You've got to understand something about Jesus while He was on Earth. Everyone says He knew everything. *He didn't know everything.*

You must realize that He laid aside all His divine privileges and walked on this planet under the Abrahamic Covenant. *He walked on*

Making a Demand on the Prophet's Anointing

this Earth like you and I do. That's the only way He could save man in the Plan of Redemption.

He had to come through a woman's womb. He had to humble Himself and walk like you and I do. He's our example, and He passed His test.

You will argue, "Yes, but He's the Son of God!"

Who do you think *you* are?

So Jesus didn't have any divine privileges when He walked on Earth unless the Father revealed things to Him supernaturally — just like He did to His other prophets. Otherwise, there were many facts about people and events Jesus wouldn't have known in the natural. But He operated in the gifts of the Spirit!

I know this isn't "religious" preaching; it's everyday living and real truth. *There is a real Jesus* — neither a statue nor a figure still hanging on the cross — a real Jesus who walked on this Earth as a human being, just like you and I walk. He felt the same infirmities you and I feel. He went through the same tests and trials we go through.

Remember when He was praying in the Garden of Gethsemane? Facing arrest and the crucifixion, He almost wanted to give up in the flesh. He prayed, *"O my Father, if it be possible, let this cup pass from me: nevertheless not as I will, but as thou wilt"* (Matthew 26:39).

Why? He was still a human being — yet He was God in the flesh!

How To Keep Your Healing

> *And his disciples said unto him, Thou seest the multitude thronging thee, and sayest thou, Who touched me?*
>
> *And he looked round about to see her that had done this thing.*
>
> *But the woman fearing and trembling, knowing what was done in her, came and fell down before him, and told him all the truth.*
>
> MARK 5:31-33

This is where a lot of people lose their healing. They don't return and testify, "I was healed when I was in your meeting the other night."

Faith That Makes a Demand on the Anointing

Jesus Sums It Up

"And He said unto her, Daughter, my being a great man of God is what healed you. My being the Son of God is what healed you. My belonging to the First Church of the 1907 Wave is what healed you. My being an elder of the First Church of Jerusalem is what healed you."

No, this is what Jesus really said to the woman (verse 34):

Daughter, *thy faith hath made thee whole;* go in peace, and be whole of thy plague.

It was her faith that did it!

And it's your faith that must make a demand on the anointing for you to get your miracle from God.

You must *believe in that anointing or mantle.*
You must *believe in the prophet of God.*
You must *release your faith.*

CONCLUSION

The only reason a person has the power to be a prophet, a pastor, or stand in any other office is because he wears the mantle of that office. God has placed that mantle on him, and if he is totally honest with himself and with you, he will admit it. It isn't his good looks that are getting him by!

When I go to a church to hold a meeting, people may think that I have a strong anointing. Yes, I take time to pray, make myself available to God, and put my flesh down. But I know that when that mantle comes on me, the anointing is in the mantle, not in me. That takes the attention away from me.

This ministry is very important to me, and it is very important to God. I'm halfway through my life, and my time is getting more and more valuable, the closer I get to my allotted age. I could just run down a prayer line, quickly touching people, but I want to do things that produce.

It's More Than a Good Time

I don't want to lay hands on people just to have a Holy Ghost nightclub, where people fall over, laugh, and have a good time.

After such services people will say, "Didn't we have a good time last night? Everyone fell on top of each other, and it was just so funny — why, the preacher told 10 jokes!"

I'd like to ask them, "Did anyone get saved? Did anyone get set free?"

That's what we're after. There is much more involved in meetings than simply having a good time. There are people in my meetings who could die with the sickness and disease they have unless they receive divine healing! That is why we must be so sensitive to the Holy Ghost.

When a man of God lays hands on you, don't just look at him; you need to see Jesus, just as if you were touching the hem of His mantle.

And when they lay hands on you, you must say, "It's finished; it's done! Amen, I believe it! That's it; I'm healed" — whether or not you have a manifestation. It doesn't matter if you have a manifestation.

I've known people who didn't feel a thing after prayer, but when they got home and went to bed, they could feel that anointing come upon them, and suddenly whatever they were suffering from left them.

We're too influenced by our five senses when it comes to divine healing. We say, "Hands were laid on me, that anointing went into me, but it still hurts."

Determined To Get a Miracle

You've got to have the same determination that was exhibited by the Shunammite woman, blind Bartimaeus, and the woman with the issue of blood. As we brought out in this book, there was just something about it — they were determined to get the miracle they sought from the prophet. They weren't going to go home without it!

As a matter of fact, the woman with the issue of blood was considered unclean, and had the crowd known of her condition, she would have been stoned to death! You talk about laying your life on the line! But she didn't have anything to lose; if she didn't get her healing, she was going to die anyway.

The anointing first came upon me in 1971 while I was attending the Full Gospel Business Men's Fellowship world convention in Denver, Colorado. It went into my right hand.

The Anointing Increases

Through the years, it has gotten stronger. Then, in 1978, Brother Kenneth E. Hagin put his arms around me during a meeting, and something else was transmitted from his prophetic man-

Conclusion

tle to mine. That's how you can increase your anointing — by being around other anointed people.

As you get more light on the subject, your faith will rise, and the anointing on you will get even stronger. So operate in faith and look to Jesus.

A man once asked me, "Where do you get all that stuff you preach?"

I said, "Don't tell anyone, but I get it from the Holy Ghost."

He knew I'm not a slick man. You see, I only have an eighth grade education, and I like to joke that the only reason I got that far is because I bribed the teacher! I'm not that smart, and I can't rely on my education, so I have to rely on God.

Some people have the natural ability to be a public speaker. Believe me, I don't. But I'd rather have the anointing on me and slur my words than be an eloquent speaker without the anointing.

For additional copies, please write to:
Ed Dufresne Ministries
P.O. Box 186
Temecula, CA 92593